A RUACH ELOHIM PARABLE

Dr. Georgette V. Prime-Godwin

The Woman At The Well
Copyright ©2014 by Georgette V. Prime-Godwin

All rights reserved. No part of this book may be reproduced, copied, stored or transmitted in any form or by any means – graphic, electronic, or mechanical, including photocopying, recording, or information storage and retrieval systems without the prior written permission of Georgette V. Prime-Godwin or HOV Publishing except where permitted by law.

Scripture quotations marked NIV are taken from the Holy Bible, New International Version. NIV. © 1973, 1978, 1984 by International Bible Society. Used by permission of Zondervan. All rights reserved. [Biblica]

HOV Publishing a division of HOV, LLC.
www.hovpub.com
hopeofvision@gmail.com

Cover Design: HOV Design Solutions

Visit the Author Dr. Georgette V. Prime-Godwin at:
www.godwininternational.org

For more information about special discounts for bulk purchases, please visit www.hovpub.com.

ISBN 978-1-942871-37-8
Library of Congress Control Number: 2018953444

10 9 8 7 6 5 4 3 2 1

Printed in the United States of America

In Loving Memory of my husband, best friend and confidante

Brian W. E. Godwin
Sunrise: July 8, 1963 – Sunset: December 19, 2014

At the beginning of this project you were there, coaching, supporting and inspiring me to finish; for this I will be forever grateful.

The word of the Lord came to me:

"Son of man, with one blow I am about to take away from you the delight of your eyes..."

Ezekiel 24:15-16, NIV

The blow was sudden. You were the picture of good health. How do I begin to recover?

Somehow you knew that the lessons penned in this book, by way of the Holy Spirit, would bring me comfort, assurance and the strength to recover.

Thank you for insisting that I finished this project with such urgency...

Always And Forever In My Heart

~

The Inglee women carried a curse that followed them from generation to generation . . .

The story of the Inglee women is a fictional tale that rings with biblical truth. The characters depicted are completely fictitious and are used to facilitate the true story, and that is forgiveness and renewal, that is found in the parable of "The Woman at the Well."

All scripture quotes have been borrowed from the New International Version of the Bible.

ACKNOWLEDGMENT

To my best friend and husband who remains at my side and constantly shows unwavering support to me and the ministry to which I have been called, to my beautiful daughter and Aunt Winnie for reading and rereading the many manuscripts, Mica for your tireless support and to my dearest friends Tyrone and Laurima, Jackie, Neville, Rev. Terry, my mother and family for your continued prayers, words of encouragement and affirmation of this project, thank you. A special thank you to Andrea, for without your guidance neither project would have become a reality.

Giving God all the honor and glory!

The Story

Content

PREFACE 15

ABOUT THE AUTHOR 16

CHAPTER 1 19

CHAPTER 2 23

CHAPTER 3 29

CHAPTER 4 34

CHAPTER 5 44

CHAPTER 6 59

CHAPTER 7 64

CHAPTER 8 77

CHAPTER 9 87

CHAPTER 10 94

EPILOGUE 101

INDEX 103

RESOURCES 111

Preface

We all have history—some good, some bad, and some that we want to forget. We must also realize that our history defines our genetic makeup. Allow the good history to determine your destiny; the bad, if unchecked, will define your character. Therefore, become a student of your history, as it will keep you from making similar mistakes; know that when you run from it, it will keep you in bondage.

When things are in our very presence, we minimize and, in most cases, discount its value. When people are right there in our midst, we take them for granted. It is only when we lose them that we appreciate their value, which is too late to reclaim.

I miss my granny Gracie's stories. I long to hear her voice again, but now it's just a distant memory.

Here's our story—the Inglee story as Granny Gracie told me . . .

Author

Rev. Dr. Georgette Prime-Godwin is an accomplished facilitator of spiritual formation, organizational leadership and business management for over 20 years. An Author and Certified Professional Life Coach, she has earned the respect of senior executives, youth and clergy personnel, having the uncanny ability to translate everyday life experiences into literal language that empowers and transforms her audiences.

Her mantra, "tiller of the earth," supports exchanges that stimulate an introspective philosophy, combined with depths of spiritual understanding, humor and personal candor—all of which are extraordinary gifts and key attributes to fueling a relaxed but attentive rapport with her participants.

A native of the beautiful Islands of Bermuda, Rev. Dr. Prime-Godwin holds a Bachelor of Science in Organizational Leadership and Management from Regent University in Virginia Beach, Virginia, a

Masters of Divinity in Pastoral Leadership from Payne Theological Seminary in Wilberforce, Ohio, an Honorary Doctorate of Divinity and Chaplaincy from CICA University and Seminary in Jamaica, New York, as well as a Certified Professional Life Coach Designation from the Life Coach Institute in Orange County, Florida.

CHAPTER 1

My name is Madeline Caroline Inglee, a fifth-generation descendant of Philomena Cassandra Marandez Inglee, my great-great-grandmother. She from modest beginnings, yet she was able to provide a solid foundation of fortitude and heroism for her descendants to follow. Sophia Cassandra Inglee, my great-grandmother, was a strong and resourceful woman. With the little that she had, she would freely give her last. She believed in family and more so in love. They tell me she was a sharp businessperson—she must have inherited it from her mother Philomena. She was able to fulfill her mother's legacy by providing the infrastructure for the well her mother set out to construct. That came at a substantial and personal cost, as she gave herself away, minute pieces at a time until she succumbed to her fate, husbandless and with an entourage of children. Grace Philomena Inglee, my grandmother, was the rock to which my anchor connected. She had a heart of gold, yet she always seemed to be carrying some sort of burden.

Granny Gracie, the eldest of Sophia's children, considered her predestined fate and, with focus and determination to rewrite the Inglee story, worked hard to find the love longed for by those before her. Gracie fulfilled the initial Inglee dream and completed the waterline for her town, but it didn't come without personal sacrifice; sometimes one has to do things against their personal conviction to see the end in view. From that encounter, Granny Gracie crossed miles of ocean with her womb full, looking for a new start, a new beginning for the one she carried. The first Inglee son was not to be; he was delivered stillborn. My mother, Caroline Marandez Inglee, was gone too soon. I inherited her name, but beyond that, all she was to me was my mother through birth. It wouldn't become clear until later that my mother passed on more than life to me.

We are strong, resourceful, and entrepreneur-minded women. All we ever wanted was to experience true love—a love that could transcend our erotic desires and emotions yet still leave our souls warm and satisfied. We seemingly struggle like most when it comes to relationships. We must have that forbidden fruit; nonetheless, he always leaves and returns to his wife. We are all named for my great-great-grandmother. I, with the exception of having my name derived from my mother, still carry a part of my great-great-grandmother having that my mom carried a part of her. It was something

The Woman At The Well

that connected us all, along with our desire for true love. Amongst our history, maybe it was the one thing we should have left in the past.

As I sit and ponder, I find myself asking, can this generational curse be broken? Can my heart find forgiveness and this love we have all yearned for? I see me in the mirror, and I affirm that, "Madeline, you are created in the image of God." I can have love; a true love that will leave me breathless yet always desiring for more. A dissimilar love than ecstasy, I search for a source of forgiveness and an agape love spoken by Him and that can only be found at the well.

My view toward life has always questioned my thoughtless actions. I consider Granny Gracie and wonder about that dark cloud that rests over her head. Many nights I stand at her door and hear her sobbing. What could cause a woman of steel to break to such sorrow? What history of the Inglee women has caused such pain?

Granny often said to me, "Lin, I must tell you the truth."

And when I questioned, "What truth?" she would often reply, "In due time, sweet pea, in due time."

What evil provokes me not to forgive? What action has gone before me that has placed shackles on my heart? Life's journey is not easy; but if you pay close attention during the process, one can learn lessons that will permit forgiveness of faults and a gauge to monitor the thought process, which determines the

> ***Lesson 1***
>
> *No matter how deep the inflicted pain is, learn to forgive.*

very essence of our foundation.

I have now found peace, for I am the woman at the well.

~

CHAPTER 2

As far back as I can remember, the Inglee women have been plagued with the curse of adultery. I recall my grandmother Gracie telling me the stories of her journey from Guyana to the paradise of the Bermuda Islands and the hardships that still seemed to follow us. This is what I remember.

It was Christmas Day, December 25, 1904, when Sophia's whole world changed. She received news that her mother, my great-great-grandmother Philomena, had been shot and killed while she stood on Platform B at the Linden Train Station as gunshots rained on the people waiting for the 6:05 p.m. train. She died soon after.

Philomena was scheduled to return home after a buying trip in Georgetown, Guyana. An astute entrepreneur with insight far beyond her years, she had purchased an old abandoned church on Skandon Street and, within a short while from the date of purchase, converted it into the home marketplace of Skeldon. She offered her clientele cloths of fine linen and cotton, ladies footwear made from local plantain leaves, grocery products, fresh fish, meats, and other produce from the local farmers. It was during this trip that Philomena was to introduce a new mechanism for retrieving water from the very depths of the earth. This apparatus looked like a barrel cut in half with a handle attached, tied with a braided cord. This new mechanism would revolutionize the township of Skeldon.

Skeldon is nestled in the alcove of the shoreline on the east coast of the North Atlantic Ocean. It boasts of a scenery seemingly only heaven could compare with, but it did not have the means of supplying those who lived inland access to fresh water. Its lush forestry, high mountains, and underground waterways of unusual fresh water were only available to those whose property bordered the natural waterfalls surrounding the outskirts of the town.

The Skeldon Township represented two predominant families, the Smiders and the Inglees. The Smiders' affluence came from *old* money. The story is told that their grandparents migrated to Guyana from Namibia then to Herero and Namaqua just after the genocide. Coming to Skeldon helped heal the fresh wounds of the genocide and it also provided a niche for the development of land for the township. They settled just along the outskirts of town where the land held more value.

Skeldon was an old, but new community, rich for development, provided one had the financial resources to invest. The Smider family had money and would soon have enough resources to purchase acres of prime real estate that would become their continuous revenue stream. They leased the property back to the businesses in the community; they sold none of their properties.

For the community, it would have been most challenging to secure such wealth, as the people who had just become emancipated were now free to commence their dreams. Money in abundance was yet to be established. The Smiders, as astute business owners, knew that posed an opportunity to help people financially, and so they created the First Bank of Skeldon, which provided financial assistance to the community for their start-up businesses.

Philomena was a refugee from Suriname, South America. Her family migrated to Skeldon for a better life. Her parents both died at an early age, leaving Philomena to care for her infirmed brother. It was a refining time. Without family, having the responsibility of caring for someone outside of herself was truly challenging. She would find herself offering washing, cooking, and care-taking services to support her and her brother. Philomena had a keen eye for detail and smarts to reckon with. Every day she had to walk miles to the waterside to retrieve water for bathing, cooking, and drinking as she lived inland. The journey would leave her brother unattended for long periods during the day. This was becoming a great concern for her, as her brother's health was rapidly deteriorating.

Philomena concluded that if a fresh water source could be erected to direct the flow inland, she could provide an infrastructure that she had witnessed on a few of her medical trips to Georgetown, Guyana. Georgetown was considered a metropolitan city during that time, and in her opinion, Skeldon could also be developed into one. Because of her acquired business acumen, she verbally surveyed several of the various mom-and-pop merchant stores and the only local physician, Dr. Jon Smider. Dr. Smider wasn't like his relatives. He chose to come and serve the people who lived on the other side of town, inland, and because of this, he was ostracized from the family fortune.

In such a small community, it wasn't uncommon for the left hand to know what the right hand was doing. It was very essential for Philomena to gain the merchants' opinion on the waterline. However, she was no fool, so she kept the intent of her questions very general as to not rouse any interest from the other Smiders, as she recognized they had the financial power to overthrow her idea. Therefore, she kept the findings of the survey very close to her chest. Funding would be critical for this project, as she recognized the necessity of having diversified revenue streams. If she could secure buy-in from her business cohorts, the newly established board under her leadership could establish a fee for the other merchants and householders to gain access to the water source. This process could provide personal financial stability for her and future generations. She had been working on this initiative for seven years and had gained enough momentum both financially and physically in support to break ground. The local merchants and other business partners were in full support of the idea. That was when she saw him.

Philip "Big Jack" Smider was of *the family* from the other side of town. When he laid eyes on Philomena, he saw a beautiful soul. He fell in love with this kind-hearted individual, but how could that be? He didn't even know her name. Even in her modest dress, he could see a woman with fortitude. After several months of observing her in the distance, Jack decided to introduce himself to her.

"Good day" were the only words he could muster as he tipped his hat in her direction.

Philomena quickly looked behind her, for this gentleman could not be speaking to her. As she gained her composure, she replied, "It is a pleasant day."

It was her voice; Jack was mesmerized. However, he had one dilemma. He knew that he could never bring her home to the family. It was bilious from his family's perspective to even speak to such people who lived on that side of town.

It had been a couple of years since Philomena's

brother had died, and her secret relationship with Jack intensified. He truly loved her, and she loved him, but she quickly surmised that it would never amount to anything true, even if she were secretly carrying his child. Jack had married the prearranged spouse. As a married man, he would have to change his focus, but he still couldn't get Philomena out of his thoughts. She was like the air for his existence. Emotionally torn, Philomena left for Georgetown three days after Jack's wedding never to return alive.

~

CHAPTER 3

When Philomena died, her untimely death left Sophia alone, frightened, and angry. Sophia sat there pondering, "How could this be?" Her mother was a very religious woman and had taught her daughter to fear God and to respect and honor the Word of God, but her mother's God let her down. After receiving the news, Sophia found herself yelling out to God and questioning, "How could you take away the only person who ever truly loved and cared for me?" All that was taught by her mother about respecting and honoring God was soon forgotten.

Sophia had golden brown skin with midnight black hair that highlighted her huge hazel brown eyes. She had a dramatic physique— hips, breasts, and a waist of uneven proportion and with an unusual height for Skeldon women. She stood 4 feet 10 inches. With the strength of her body, she could spear a wild boar, and carry it the distance from the jungle to her home, which was no easy feat, as it was a staggering 13 mile one-way trip. Even with her masculinity, when seen in her most feminine apparel, her beauty was every bit noticeable. She was a legend with men. Many came and went. She was attracted to married men, however, she never married. Her rationale was a married man came without commitment or baggage.

> *Lesson 2*
>
> *You represent the temple of God. Honor the place where the Spirit of God dwells.*

After desperately trying to fill the void of her mother's death, Sophia would find herself in the arms of different men for sensual gratification, never to be fulfilled. There was one suitor, William Straetor. He would call on her and could rouse the deepest recesses of her desires, but more importantly, he understood her. William was a man of meager beginnings with the determination for acquiring success like a tiger awaiting its prey. He was the sixth child of William Scanlon Straetor Sr. and Lucille Sarai Smider. Although William Sr. married into the Smider family, Lucille's parents and her older siblings never received him or any of their children, as they didn't come from good stock. William Sr. was the collector of Skeldon's raw sewage. His work provided an avenue that intertwined within the elite social circles. He was responsible for cleaning up human and animal excrement. In those days, the work was manual, with a sanitary horse-drawn cart going from house to house, business to business, cleaning and emptying the outside commodes. The treatment he received when he came to the affluent side of Skeldon was as if *he* was the excrement, except for Lucille, who saw him first as a man. Lucille was a homely looking individual; she never carried herself as if she was wealthy.

> **Lesson 3**
> *Your job can never define who you are. It provides a means to an end, so just work at it with integrity.*

Granny Gracie said, "I believe she wanted out and latched on to the first man she saw."

William Sr. was someone to look at, but the connection with Lucille just didn't seem compatible. Unfortunately, even with an affluent bloodline, their children were treated no different than William Sr.

William Jr. couldn't get enough of Sophia. She intrigued him. He was of dark-skinned complexion and piercing brown eyes. William was any woman's dream. He stood 6 feet 4 inches tall with a clad iron physique. William's wife was just as strikingly beautiful. William was a devoted husband, but still had a weakness and a strong yearning for Sophia. It was March 4, 1944, when Sophia called on William. As my granny Gracie recalled the story, "It was the night of the fiercest hurricane to ever hit the shoreline of Skeldon. Two hundred people lost their lives, and one life was conceived that night, and that was mine."

Skeldon carried similar attributes as any small community; it was too intimate. There was common intimacy and the community was stagnant, toxic, and claustrophobic. By the time Gracie was eighteen, Sophia had given birth to 10 children, each having different fathers. Gracie was the eldest.

Gracie considered the Inglee history, for she knew her mother wanted out, but could never find the open door. Her mother was husbandless and charged with the 10 bastard children she brought into the world. Gracie had one indiscretion, which placed her in a similar position as her mother, Sophia. Not desiring to follow in her mother's footsteps, Gracie became transfixed to scribe her own history. She desired much more for her life. When the opportunity presented itself, at twenty-three years of age with her womb full, she left on the *Bermuda Vesellé*, a mini- yacht, charted to leave Skeldon, Guyana, for the islands of Bermuda.

Gracie soon realized her inability to adapt to life on the unpredictable Atlantic Ocean. No one or nothing could have equipped her for this horrendous trip by boat to the island of Bermuda. The ocean seemed to be angry at life, as the yacht dipped in the grandest of waves. Severe seasickness was inevitable and resulted in her body being unable to care for her first child. On the ocean, he did not have a fighting chance. The only saving grace for her was the stories she heard of Bermuda. It was described as the one stop between heaven and earth. This trip took 43 days and 43 nights.

The Woman At The Well

There were some good days and bad ones, with picturesque sunsets and, on one occasion, an unusual sunrise, where both the moon and the sun displayed their harmony while sharing the same sky. And on the other hand, the swells kept her perched at the yacht's siding. There was one occasion Granny described the majesty of God, as the moon surrendered to the sun and the sunlight filled the heavens, its rays exposing the heavens. As she reflected that beautiful moment, as Granny Gracie could only describe it, she would say, "The sight was absolutely breathtaking!"

~

CHAPTER 4

When Gracie arrived in Bermuda, the stories she heard provided no justice for what she saw. Bermuda was more beautiful than she could have ever imagined. With its majestic pink coral shorelines, protected reefs, and with the bluest of crystal clear waters, she exclaimed, "This must be heaven!"

The people were very warm and hospitable and, of course, could sense the newcomer to the community. The berth was in St. George, the capital. It bustled with activity. It felt like Skeldon, but was different as no one seemed to be

> **Lesson 4**
> *You are the composer with a pen. Begin transcribing your destiny.*

interested in the personal affairs of another. Gracie

had already purchased accommodations before leaving Skeldon, as it was part of her one-way boarding package on the *Veselle*. No one with a one-way ticket was allowed extended stay on the island unless they had secured proper and fitting long-term lodgings.

Gracie used her entire savings to purchase the one-way passage to the island of Bermuda. Her home was meager, yet it was comfortable. It was located in Tucker's Estate, an area overlooking the south shore. It sat on three acres of arable land, so Gracie immediately went to work and planted various crops and soon provided enough to be sold at the market. Grace Inglee's name was synonymous to business gurus, and soon, she took people into her confidence and provided successful business tips to them. These tips, of course, came with a fee. Gracie was only on the island 18 months, and she had established a market to service those who lived on the western and central parts of the island. This placed her in a very comfortable financial position and also a promotion into the elite social circles.

It was at the governor's ball when she first noticed him. A strikingly handsome, fair-skinned, dark-haired gentleman, he wasn't as tall as she would have liked, but with his European physique—broad shoulders and narrow waist—she couldn't help staring. He was seemingly engaged in conversation with a few other gentlemen, but he noticed her also. Gracie's physique was a cross between American Indian and

African American. Her skin was like dark molted chocolate, her eyes were a peculiar hazel green, and her dark brown hair was short and curly. There was no excess flesh on her, everything was well proportioned, and her smile radiated a set of beautiful snow-white teeth.

There was a brief eye exchange between her and the gentleman across the dance floor before Albert, the governor's aide, whisked her off for a dance. She was of average height, so that whoever she danced with, and if over 5 feet 11 inches, made her fit within their torso like a hand in a glove.

As she was dancing with Albert, she had to ask him, "Who was the gentleman in the dark gray zoot suit?"

"Who, Jeffrey Sandyman?" Albert replied. "Sandyman, that's a peculiar name," she replied.

"Gracie, stay away from him. He's—" Just as Albert was completing his sentence, the governor made his exit. "I have to go," said Albert. "We can chat later."

As the night progressed, Gracie really couldn't help it. Every time she saw Jeffrey, her body would respond in such a way that she knew in her heart was wrong. "But it's just a feeling," she convinced herself.

It was time to call it a night, and she left before trouble could find her.

Although Albert wasn't her type, she needed comfort, and at least she knew him. Albert's visits were very frequent, and he was falling for her, yet Gracie wouldn't have it. Albert was the perfect gentleman, but she wanted Jeffrey. She hadn't laid eyes on him since the governor's ball and found it to be inappropriate to ask Albert of his whereabouts.

Life continued. It had been a year since the governor's ball when she was invited to another elitists' event in the west end of the island. Jeffrey was there. He wore a black satin zoot suit with the grandfather clock pendant hanging from his top pocket, with penguin leather shoes that you could see your reflection. He nodded in her direction, and she gave a blushful response. He did have someone on his arms.

"Not important," she whispered to herself.

Albert came over to her at that moment and asked, "Do you want a drink?" as he passed her a glass of champagne.

The night was really uneventful, but definitely an eye-opener, as it provided Gracie with the latest gossip in the elite community. She quickly discovered that the lady on Jeffrey's arm was in fact his wife. They were both great with making public appearances, but their relationship was very strained behind closed doors.

As she sat alone at the bar, she felt someone standing behind her. She knew it was him without even turning around.

"Good evening, my lady," he said.

His voice sent a shudder down her spine. It was smooth, sensuous, and inviting. With every bit of composure that she could muster, she slowly turned and returned the cordiality. "And good evening to you, Jeffrey Sandyman."

"So, this is unfair, as you know my name and I don't know yours," he replied.

With an extended hand, she replied, "My name is Grace Inglee. My friends call me Gracie."

"Inglee?" he questioned. "That's not a local name."

"No, I migrated from Skeldon, Guyana," she replied.

He chuckled as he responded, "So, how long have you been in Bermuda 'cause you don't have much of an accent."

She never got to respond, as Albert came over to interrupt the conversation. "Jeffrey!", he said in a very cold manner.

"Albert!" Jeffrey responded in the same tone.

"Gracie, are you ready to leave?" Albert asked as he gently placed his hand on her lower back.

In Gracie's thoughts, she wanted to leave, but not with him. Something came up in her, and she said to Albert, "No, I'm not ready to leave, but if you must go, feel free to leave." She knew Albert had to report to work at the police station at midnight.

Albert whispered in her ear, "Be careful," and left.

Jeffrey was so captivated by Gracie. Initially, he could only admire her from a distance. Now, up close and personal, he noticed her skin looked so soft. He wanted to reach out and touch her. *"She is so beautiful,"* he thought.

Her dress was opal white and fit her in all of the right places and accentuated her dark complexion. The back provided a deep plunge that exposed her lower back. He had to hold her.

"Gracie, can we have this dance?" Jeffrey asked.

> **Lesson 5**
>
> *You may strongly desire it and perhaps even enjoy it. But as long as it belongs to someone else, it can never be yours.*

She responded with all modesty, "I do believe it to be inappropriate to dance with a married man." "I'm not married. We are currently in divorce proceedings," he responded.

"But the lady that I saw you with—" Gracie began to say as he gently placed his warm hand on her lower back. Mesmerized, she got up and found herself in his arms. They danced and danced the night away. He offered to take her home, and she conceded.

The next morning, Gracie awoke to an empty bed, but his aroma was still fresh on the pillow and sheets. It was a wonderful night; she had never felt that way in any of her encounters. She put on her robe and wandered out to the kitchen. It was a beautiful Bermuda morning. The sky seemed bluer than usual and the breeze felt cooler than it ever had been in the peak of summer. She noticed a small card on the edge of the table.

You are beautiful. I would like to see you again this evening. Dinner at the Victoria Hotel. See you at 7:00 p.m.

Jeffrey

Gracie was beside herself and spent the whole day trying to determine what she would wear to this special occasion. She was trying not to convince herself that she was falling in love. Her heart was speaking very loudly, "I truly love this man."

The relationship seemed to bloom over the next few months. Jeffrey had even partially moved in. Whenever Gracie asked when the divorce was to be final, Jeffrey always made excuses. They were very compatible in bed and socially, but something was different. Jeffrey seemed to drink more and would only stay if she pressured him to do so.

She would ask, "Jeffrey, where do you go when you are not with me?"

He would only become agitated. She learned quickly not to ask because when she did he would pack up and leave.

"I will not pressure him," she murmured.

One evening, as Gracie was at home waiting for Jeffrey to show up, there was a knock on the door. Gracie sang out, "I'm coming!"

Anticipating Jeffrey, she had put on the sheer teddy he admired her in with the silk bathrobe he had given her the last time they made up after a nasty fight. She ran to open the door.

"Albert?" she said sheepishly as she tried to recompose herself. "Albert, what are you doing here?" she asked.

"May I come in?" he asked.

She responded, "For a short moment, I'm

expecting company." "Thank you," he replied.

Albert had to work the graveyard shift, as he also served as a police reserve officer. "Gracie," he spoke, and it was hardly audible.

Gracie felt a knot in her stomach. "Albert?" she responded just as quietly. "Bermuda has recorded its first murder."

Gracie found herself screaming at the top of her lungs, calling for Jeffrey. "Jeffrey, is he—oh please, God, not Jeffrey!" she cried.

Albert looked confused. "Ah, Gracie, Adele committed the murder." "What!" she exclaimed.

"She shot Jeffrey at point blank range in the chest. I am here because she is looking for you."

"Why is she looking for me?" Gracie asked.

"Gracie, Jeffrey was married to a known psychopath." "A psychopath!" she repeated in horror.

"Yes, the night I whispered in your ear 'Be careful,' you were already on her hit list."

"Oh, my God! What do I do?"

"We have two squad cars patrolling the neighborhood, and I volunteered to be stationed here with you." Then he asked, "Would you like a drink?"

"Surely," she replied.

Albert had been hearing rumors of Jeffrey and his Gracie, but thought them to be only rumors.

How could... When did... Why would Gracie react in such a manner when she heard of Jeffrey's death? he grimaced.

The thought of Gracie and Jeffrey sickened him, but he still loved her and even wanted her now.

Gracie's home remained under police surveillance for a few weeks. Jeffrey's wife hadn't been found, nor was there any indication that she was still after Gracie.

During this time, while she was secretly mourning the death of Jeffrey, her and Albert's relationship had rekindled. It was good to have someone around, as it truly helped ease the pain.

Bermuda experienced a freak storm late October. It had rained continuously for one week; there were flooded pockets of terrain all over the island. Both Albert and Gracie had a lovely dinner and turned in as the power went out due to the storm. As Gracie lay in the alcove of Albert, she had this uncanny feeling that they were being watched. She denounced the feeling, for she was tired. Maybe her conscience was agitated, for that night marked the anniversary of Jeffrey's death. Perhaps it was a hunch. She looked at Albert as he was engaged in his rhythmic snoring. Gracie began to doze just as Albert stopped snoring.

The bang was so loud that it blocked out the sound of the rainstorm. Gracie felt something warm embracing her. With the lights still out from the storm, Gracie gently knocked Albert, as he sounded like he was moaning. Then there was an unfamiliar female voice that spoke in a loud audible whisper, "You will never have my Jeffrey, and now you won't have Albert."

There was another bang and then silence. The silence was just as loud as the bang. Amazingly, the electricity returned, and the side lamp became lit.

"Oh God! Oh God!" Gracie found herself screaming.

Albert lay beside her, with half of his face blown off. The warmth she felt was blood. It was Albert's blood. She was covered in Albert's blood. She proceeded to run out to call the police when she fell over something.

"I've seen her before," Gracie mumbled.

But why was this woman in her house? Why did she come to her house to shoot herself? Now she is dead on her floor. Why would she kill Albert? Gracie had so many questions. As she looked around, there was so much blood—it was everywhere.

Gracie was able to call for help. When the police arrived, they transported her to the hospital for observation. As she was recuperating from the shock, the police advised that the woman on the floor of her house was the late Adele Smider, Jeffrey Sandyman's wife.

Bermuda recorded its first murder-suicide.

~

CHAPTER 5

Life in Bermuda suddenly shifted for Gracie. Her focus was now less on self-desire and more on work, work, and more work. She tended her many gardens and business was great. With her profits, she renovated her home, installing an indoor toilet and a white, steel, claw-foot tub. She converted her dining room into a green house. Gracie had a green thumb, finger, and hand. Everything she touched bloomed and blossomed.

Gracie found her religion once again and began attending the Lightning Tabernacle Church. Its services were vibrant, with lively music, and the community was just the right

> ***Lesson 6***
>
> *Trust God before man. You will never be disappointed.*

combination to help with her healing.

She plunged herself in the ministry of the church and was involved in the choir, served on the usher board, and helped with the children's church. She was at her church from sunup to sundown. When someone said they couldn't make it, it was no problem for Gracie. She availed herself to her church.

Her activity and dedication didn't go unnoticed. The pastor, Rev. Absalom Bultner, was most appreciative of Gracie's service. He also noticed her beauty. Whenever he saw her, something about her aroused his sensuality. Reverend Bultner had served as senior pastor of the church for five years. Although he was the senior pastor, he was a young man. He was tall, had light-brown-skinned, and curly black hair. For a guy with large hands and feet, his demeanor was quiet. However, there was something about the pastor that made Gracie uncomfortable so she always made it a point to never be in his presence alone.

One Sunday after service, Gracie was packing up the hymnals and Bibles, her typical duties after a worship service, and inadvertently, she found herself in the sanctuary alone with the pastor. He approached her from behind. "Sister Gracie, I would like to personally thank you for your commitment to the ministry here at Lightning Tabernacle."

Startled, Gracie answered, "Pastor, it is a pleasure to serve."

"Absalom," he responded. "You can call me, Absalom." "Okay, Absalom. It is a pleasure to serve."

They continued their light conversation. "You are

a beautiful woman, Gracie," said Absalom.

"Thank you," responded Gracie. "If there's nothing else," Gracie stated, "I'll be going."

Before she could turn and leave, he had reached for her and was on top of her. The shock kept her from screaming. He had his way with her and left her lying on the church floor.

Gracie left that church and *the* church and never looked back.

A few months after that episode with Absalom, Gracie noticed that whenever she ate her favorite foods, it always made her nauseous. After Natalie, a member of Lightning Tabernacle, encouraged a doctor's visit, Gracie soon found out that she was pregnant—a constant reminder of that day and Absalom Bultner. Gracie hated that man, and the fact that he was a pastor only solidified her feelings.

In the fall of 1968, Gracie gave birth to a beautiful baby girl, Caroline Marandez Inglee, five pounds two ounces. The fourth-generation descendant of Philomena Cassandra Marandez Inglee, granddaughter to Sophia Cassandra Inglee, and daughter to Gracie Philomena Inglee.

After the birth of Caroline, Gracie became introverted, and she refused to attend the elitist social events. She felt cursed. Everyone that she truly loved died. She began to reminisce. When Jeffrey was killed, she knew she could never love another man as she did him. And then there was Albert; her love for him was rooted in a deep friendship and not with the erotic passion that only Jeffrey aroused in her. Even her good friend Sister Natalie Krisler died prematurely. She was only in her mid-thirties when she succumbed to an acute bout of the shingles.

When Gracie thought of her good friend Natalie, she remembered it was difficult to remain in contact with her. It had little to do with Natalie; for she was the sweetest person Gracie had ever met. Natalie had tried on several occasions to get in contact with Gracie, but she would have no part of it, as it reminded her of the dreadful day at Lightning Tabernacle.

Gracie was determined to take that story to her grave. That was until her only daughter Caroline inadvertently introduced her to Nahshon Bultner Jones.

Despite the circumstance that led to the conception and birth of Caroline, Gracie could only see the most beautiful little girl to ever live. As Caroline matured, Gracie noticed that her stature remained small, bordering on frail. She was not like the typical Inglee women; her physique seemed to ail with some sort of sickness. When she was about twelve years of age, Gracie was forced to take her to the hospital where she was diagnosed with hypertrophic cardiomyopathy—a disease of the heart muscle. Her heart muscle was abnormally thick, making it harder for it to pump blood. It was important for Caroline to limit activity as to not place extra stress on her heart.

Gracie was able to provide the necessary care and shelter for Caroline, but she was an independent spirit, and no one would have known the seriousness of her health based on her activeness. Caroline found strength in the church. She would always invite her mother to accompany her, but for whatever reason, Gracie would always find an excuse why she couldn't go.

Caroline found that the only place where she felt whole was when she was working in the church, and so she sang in the choir and served in the pastor's cabinet. She thought the world of Pastor Absalom Bultner. He was kind and often demonstrated favor for women in ministry. Caroline had answered the call to ministry and was set to begin her studies.

Pastor Bultner, now in his late 50s, still hadn't come to grips with his previous indiscretions or even prayed for forgiveness. The one characteristic he possessed was forgetting. He believed what was done in the past should stay there. Throughout his ministry, he seemed to be in and out of encounters, the last one was with a parishioner on one of his pastoral visitations.

Sis. Claudia Jones, a widow, sought counsel through her church, Lightning Tabernacle. Her initial visitations included Sis. Caroline Inglee with Pastor Absalom Bultner. The visits were enriching and focused on assisting Sister Jones to migrate back into society. Sister Jones was married for only a year when her husband died of prostate cancer. Pastor Bultner had decided when he entered the ministry to be a groom to the church; in other words, he would dedicate his life to the ministry. This stance did not provide opportunity for marriage in the natural state.

However, Pastor Bultner's visitations became more frequent and more outside the auguries of the church's by-laws, which stated when the pastor conducts visitations with members of the opposite sex, a female cabinet member must accompany the pastor. Although Caroline served in the pastor's cabinet, she was not the only female who did. There were two other females, both who had independently and unknowingly experienced copulation with the pastor. It became an accepted norm, but for some peculiar reason, he never saw Caroline in that capacity. It had been approximately a year since the formal counsel sessions began between Sister Jones and Pastor Bultner. The relationship between them had bloomed into a relationship, a partnership that could benefit the ministry of the church. Nahshon was the son of Sister Jones. When she and Pastor Bultner married, and within the year of their marriage, he adopted Nahshon. They named him Nahshon Bultner Jones. Caroline left Bermuda to further her education in Canada at the headquarters of Spirit and Faith Church Inc. She held fast to the call which was on her life and was diligent in her studies. She had learned to live with her disease and would be careful not to engage in any exercise that would place additional pressure on her heart.

    There was a healing revival that came to the campus, which intrigued Caroline. The presence of God was truly present and she accepted the fact that she was healed and even called home to express the same with her mother.

    "Mom!" Caroline shouted over the telephone.

    Immediately, when Gracie heard her daughter's voice, she was full of anxiety. "Lin, what's wrong?" She affectionately called her Lin for short.

"Nothing is wrong, Mother—everything is so right. I received my healing tonight at the revival!" exclaimed Caroline. "I am so excited I ran over to the dorm to call you. Mother, I ran to the dorm, and I feel fine!" Caroline shouted gleefully.

"That is wonderful news!" said Gracie, not wanting to ward off her enthusiasm. "Please be careful, Lin," her mother cautioned.

They continued to express simple pleasantries until their call ended.

Gracie became gravely concerned. It had been so long since she believed in faith, the church, and even God. She didn't want anything to happen to her Lin, so just before she went to bed, she said a quiet prayer, "Dear God, please keep your hand of protection on my baby, in Jesus's name. Amen."

Caroline would spend the next five years studying and doing her practicum at Spirit and Faith Church Inc. and in two weeks, her mother would be there to celebrate her graduating top of her class. She had no desire to return to Bermuda after her graduation and that conversation she would have in person with her mother after graduation. Gracie was faced with a dilemma, for she had to obtain permission from her doctor to travel to Caroline's graduation. It was only three weeks prior to Caroline's graduation invitation when Gracie was diagnosed with isolated systolic hypertension. She was only able to travel if the prescribed medication worked to lower her levels. Gracie was diagnosed a few years earlier with a touch of hypertrophic cardiomyopathy.

Even with such a diagnosis, Gracie's constitution was exceptionally strong and she hadn't had any health challenges until now. The doctor claimed that her current symptoms were the result of stress. What was bothering her? She had no clue, but the one thing she knew, she would not miss her daughter's graduation for anything.

Back on the home front in Bermuda, Gracie heard that Pastor Bultner had suffered a severe heart attack and died. His funeral arrangements were pending. In the meantime, his son Nahshon Bultner Jones was appointed as the acting overseer at Lightning Tabernacle until a pastor could be reassigned.

The graduation was absolutely breathtaking. While Gracie reminisced of Lin crossing the stage with her Master of Theology degree and the pride she felt, her thoughts had completely drowned out Caroline's statement of not returning to Bermuda.

"Mom, are you okay with me staying here in Canada for a while?" Caroline beckoned.

"Lin, you have been away from me for so long. I had great plans for us back home. How long were you planning on staying?"

Caroline then saw her mother in a whole different light, she looked aged. "Mom, we can go back together. I can put my plans on hold for at least another year," she said.

Caroline returned home and soon became involved in the ministry of Lightning Tabernacle. She was devastated that Pastor Bultner had passed and quite frustrated that headquarters would not appoint her as the new pastor. She was qualified. Nahshon, in her opinion, lacked the drive for the ministry to actually lead it.

Caroline found herself trying to coach Nahshon on how to facilitate the ministry so that God's glory was felt in the sanctuary. Instead, he would listen, but never follow the advice of Caroline. He had a purpose for his madness. He found Caroline attractive, and the only way that he could remain in her presence was to act ineffective so that they could have continuous interaction regarding the ministry.

It had been a long time since Caroline had experienced any signs of her illness. By faith, she was healed, however, since she was back home, she began experiencing ever-so-slight chest pains and shortness of breath. She hadn't been out to church and Nahshon had become concerned. He decided on Monday, May 24, a holiday, to visit Caroline at her home. Gracie had decided, with Caroline's persuasion, to go to the holiday parade.

Nahshon had arrived unannounced at Caroline's home. Since she felt comfortable around Nahshon, she invited him in the house. They spoke of superficial pleasantries and some church concerns. Caroline had never known a man. Nahshon finally built up enough nerve and said to Caroline, "You are so beautiful."

Caroline quickly responded, "No need to flatter me, I am just plain ole Caroline, interested in the work of the ministry."

Without any warning, Nahshon took Caroline and left her breathless and stripped her of her womanhood. When Gracie came home, she sensed something different about Caroline, but neither spoke of what they felt nor what had happened.

Caroline laid about the house despondent. She had no drive to go to church nor did she care about the ministry. She continuously questioned herself, "What did I do? Why would he do this to me?"

Gracie kept watch over Lin from a distance and thought, *"She doesn't want to go to church? What is keeping her here in this house?"*

"The secret of her father and her birth would never be discussed," Gracie had declared twenty-six years earlier.

It had been just as long since she had placed foot inside Lightning Tabernacle Church. She was determined to uncover what had happened at the church that was keeping her daughter from attending. It was hard to walk into that sanctuary. A place where one should find peace and healing, Gracie only felt hatred and betrayal as she stood in the exact spot, for not much had changed since she was last there. As she was lost in her thoughts, a man's voice echoed. "Good day. May I help you?"

Startled, she replied, "Yes, I am looking for the person who is in charge of this assembly."

"That would be me," he answered.

Gracie couldn't believe the resemblance in demeanor and had to ask, "Are you— I'm sorry, were you related to the former pastor?"

"Yes, Pastor Absalom was my father," he said as he extended his hand. "My name is Nahshon Bultner Jones."

Gracie stood frozen and did not reciprocate the

handshake. Puzzled by the response, Nahshon asked, "How can I help you?"

"My name is Gracie Inglee, mother of Caroline Inglee. I am here to uncover why my daughter doesn't want to come to church. Do you know why?"

Now Nahshon had the same characteristic as his father—forgetting; he had long forgotten the encounter with Caroline. He responded, "I'm not sure. I think you will need to have that conversation with her."

Caroline's genetics carried the Inglee fortitude gene, and she decided it was time to face Nahshon as she noticed that she was very late with her menstrual cycle, three months late to be exact. She mustered up every bit of strength that she had and went to the church, unannounced, to see Nahshon. When she arrived, he was stunned to see her, as it was evident by the look on his face when she entered the deacon board meeting. Everyone was excited to see her. Nahshon seemed confused to see her.

"What could she want?" He thought.

"May I speak to Nahshon alone?" she asked the board. They left immediately and closed the door behind them.

"I have been going over and over in my mind, did I lead you on? Did I deserve this kind of treatment?" Caroline exclaimed. "You sit here, leading this ministry like you have done nothing wrong!"

Nahshon quickly jumped to his feet, shouting, "You wanted it as much as I did!"

"You are a self-centered bastard!" Caroline

shouted. "You come to my house, on the pretense of a church visit, to rape me!" She was screaming now. Although she had asked the deacon board to be excused, they were in the sanctuary listening to the conversation. "You will pay for this!" Caroline shouted.

Nahshon shouted back, "It is your word over mine!"

"Well, it would be more than a word. I am pregnant! You will confront the deacon board and relieve yourself of your responsibilities!" shouted Caroline.

And with that, she stormed out of the office, right past the deacon board and never looked back.

It was time to advise her mother. Her decision to keep the pregnancy, even though the likelihood of death for her would be imminent, was the most difficult thing she had ever encountered. There should be no pregnancy with her state of heart disease, yet she would not terminate the unplanned pregnancy. When Caroline explained to Gracie her current condition, Gracie could only cry out with the deepest pain. Even though the pain was so close to her own, she would not tell Lin the origin of her life. Not only was he the father of Lin's unborn child, but he was also her stepbrother.

Caroline died giving birth to me, Madeline Caroline Inglee. I weighed in at a healthy 6 pounds 11

Lesson 7

Decisions can have long-lasting effects. Always consider your decisions.

ounces.

Silence became the author of the late Caroline's family and Reverend Nahshon's indiscretion until two years later, when he became involved with Deacon Burtney Brown's only daughter, Briden Nathalie Brown. Briden was a beautiful young Christian lady, the jewel of Deacon Brown's eye. Deacon Brown had lost his wife to cancer shortly after Briden was born, and as a father, he tried to do everything right by his daughter. She was raised in an environment that emphasized the importance of self-restraint, but Briden was far from celibate. Her secret relationship with Rev. Nahshon Bultner Jones was about to become public—she was pregnant.

Deacon Brown had served on the board that dreadful day when the late Caroline Inglee accused Reverend Nahshon of her pregnancy. The board did not want to cause bad public relations within the community they served, and so they sided with the pastor and kept that incident behind closed doors. Now Deacon Brown would once again be caught up in a pastor-and-parishioner indiscretion, and this time it was too close to home.

Soon after Briden found out she was carrying Reverend Nahshon's child, she approached him with the news as she desired nothing less than to be a wife of a pastor and was assured that her pregnancy would present her with such favor. However, Reverend Nahshon wasn't so convinced that the child was his and flatly refused to engage in a marriage just because some woman claimed to be carrying his child.

When Briden told her father that she was

The Woman At The Well

pregnant, it totally broke his heart, but when she told her father that Reverend Nahshon was the father, his brokenness turned into hate and destruction.

"Oh no! I'll be damned if he will do this to another family!" he shouted.

"Daddy!" Briden cried out to him as she had never before seen her father so enraged.

Her father disappeared into the basement for about 20 minutes. As he ascended from the basement, she couldn't believe her eyes. "Daddy . . . no!" she screamed.

Deacon Brown took his hunting revolver and headed toward Lightning Tabernacle Church.

As Deacon Brown approached the church, he noticed one familiar car in the parking lot and then proceeded through the sanctuary and busted through the pastor's study door. All three stood frozen in their actions.

"Deacon Mitchel, what the hell is going on here? Why are you on your knees? Reverend Nahshon, have you lost your god-forsaken mind? You are doing this here in the church's office?" shouted Deacon Brown as he took his revolver and pointed it toward the pastor.

"Mitchel, get the hell out of here!" yelled Deacon Brown.

Reverend Nahshon tried to reason with Deacon Brown. "It's not what it looks like!"

"Not what it looks like? You try explaining why when I came into this office I see two grown men in such close proximity with each other, fixing or unfixing each other's clothes? You hypocritical bastard! You couldn't just settle with impregnating my daughter . . . and you are also—" Deacon Brown couldn't bring himself to finish the statement when Briden burst into the office.

"Daddy, please put the gun down!" Briden begged her father.

Deacon Brown was totally broken. He had held the pastor in such high regard, and now this. His hand was still fixed on the trigger with the barrel only inches away from the pastor.

"Daddy, please, I love him!" cried Briden.

"You don't love him, you can't love him!" shouted Deacon Brown. "Please, Daddy!" begged Briden as she cried uncontrollably.

From the yelling she had heard and the way Deacon Mitchel ran past her, she always had a hunch that there was someone else. Despite that, she loved Pastor Nahshon Bultner Jones and, somehow, she was going to marry him, no matter what her father felt.

Rev. Nahshon Bultner Jones and Briden Nathalie Brown were married. Nine months later, they gave birth to Musalem Bultner Jones, a healthy and beautiful 7-pound, 10-ounce baby boy.

~

CHAPTER 6

Whenever my granny would begin to tell our story, it would prove to be a very long-winded event.

"Granny, I have to go," I said. I really had nowhere to go, but I would do anything not to hear the same old story again. Granny was old, in her early 90s, and sooner or later, she would start talking about God, the church, the well—just not today! A few of my friends were going to hang out at Duffie's Hideaway in Hamilton. This place had a television, not any type of television, but one that was in color. It was limited in color, as everything had an orangey tint to it. It was covered with orange cellophane wrap. The reception wasn't that good. We were able to see the picture only when Michael would stand and hold the makeshift antenna—a wire hanger. The plan was to hang out there for a while and then go down to the beach and create a bonfire, sit around, drink root beer and ginger beer sodas, and eat roasted marshmallows.

I loved living in Bermuda, with its pink coral beachfronts and crystal-clear, blue water. The island of Bermuda, a British colony, was the place my grandmother Gracie considered a safe haven to raise me, her only granddaughter. Granny Gracie always told me how special I was, and I held a sacredness of truth that only Mary, Jesus's mother, had. I was well aware of my peculiarity and would often find myself running a path to nowhere, just running, trying to escape this invisible force. Now this force, mind you, had kept me from getting involved with the neighborhood gang, of which I was eternally grateful. Those gang members received a double-life sentence without parole for their participation in the hold-up at a store on Montpelier Street at gunpoint. The storeowner died at the scene. There was another time in a dream that I felt engulfed by the invisible force and I had shared this weird dream with Granny Gracie.

> **Lesson 8**
>
> *Learn to cherish sharedmoments, for it is most difficult to reclaim that which is gone.*

Between the time that I had left Granny's to go and hangout with my friends, the neighbor's son, Musalem, popped by as he often did to visit Granny. When he arrived, Granny didn't look well.

"Musalem, will you fix me a hot cup of tea? And would you mind, dear, fetching Madeline. I really

The Woman At The Well

need to speak with her. I believe she's at the beach with her friends," she said, grimacing while holding her left arm.

Granny began to rub her upper left shoulder to move the trapped gas. Musalem asked, "Granny, are you all right?"

"Yes, I'm fine," she muttered. "I just can't seem to move this... gas." She was just about to tell Musalem to go, as she encountered an unbearable pain in her arm. After Musalem left, Granny called on the Lord as she had continuously done before over the last fifty years. "Please, Lord, just allow me to tell Madeline the story. Before I go, I need the curse to be broken. Amen," said Granny.

The pain intensified. Granny willed herself to remain alert until I arrived.

Musalem found me at the beach with my friends. Initially, I refused to leave my friends, but Musalem would not take no for an answer. We left together and headed toward the house. Musalem was the son of Nahshon Bultner Jones. Granny insisted that I refer to his dad as Uncle Nahshon, but I refused to accept Nahshon as my uncle. I do not know why, but there was something I didn't like about Nahshon's character. I did not trust him and I could never determine why I felt that way.

"Call him uncle, that would be a cold day in hell," I muttered under my breath.

Musalem was special and I truly loved him. He was a generous and kind individual who always seemed to be around when I really needed a friend. We were like kindred spirits.

As we headed back to the house, I asked Musalem, "What is wrong with my granny?"

Musalem responded, "Lin," he affectionately called me, "your granny isn't feeling well. She is very adamant that she has to speak with you now."

When we arrived at the house, Granny Gracie was sleeping. Granny looked so peaceful as I stood at the foot of the bed looking over her. Although Granny seemed as though she was resting, the Holy Spirit had her mind engaged, reflecting on the dream I had shared with her so long ago:

It was dusk. The area was unfamiliar with people running, they were running everywhere. Everyone was running. I was running. They were all running from something in the far distance. It had a sunset-colored glow and it resembled a huge tumbleweed. As it moved toward me, it caught up with and rolled over the people, consuming everything in sight. As I ran, the tumbleweed was getting larger and strangely hotter the closer it got to me. In front of me was a river and behind me this tumbleweed was engulfed in fire.

"If I could only make it to the river," granny remembers me saying.

I looked back and the huge tumbleweed was only a few feet away. The atmosphere was becoming increasingly hot and there was no one left. I was left running alone and then the hot tumbleweed consumed my foot and then my leg. Then I was totally engulfed in this burning tumbleweed, frantically trying to get out of it. This invisible force held me in its grip and I stopped running as I realized the burning tumbleweed was not burning my clothing, skin, nor hair. There was a comforting warmth I felt deep within, and it gently forced me to be still. I heard an unforgettable voice, which I described to Granny.

It said, *"I am that I am.*[1] *Madeline, I have called you to be an agent for me. I am the Alpha and the Omega, the beginning and the end.*[2]*"*

Granny Gracie awakened to see her beautiful granddaughter standing at the foot of the bed with tears flowing down her cheeks.

~

---

[1] Exodus 3:14
[2] Revelation 21:6

CHAPTER 7

"I must tell Madeline the story *that will free her from all her fears and, most importantly, eradicate the Inglee curse,"* Granny Gracie concluded in her thoughts.

In a feeble voice, she called me to come near. "Sit here," she said as she placed her hand on the side of the bed. "My Madeline, I must tell you *the story*," Granny said.

"Granny, please get some sleep, I've heard the story before," I said. Granny placed her hand on her mouth, indicating for me to stop talking and to listen. "I need to tell you *the story*. God has given me one

last chance to tell it and break it. Madeline, I should have told you sooner . . .," she said as her memory reflected that dreadful day at Lightning Tabernacle.

The Woman At The Well

I was convinced that Granny was probably hallucinating or maybe Musalem gave her some medication, for she was making no sense. I gave Granny the Inglee look and said, "I need you to rest and we can talk later."

> **Lesson 9**
>
> *You have a built-in resistance to failure, a strength that propels you forward. For you are created in the image of God.*

With all the strength Granny could muster, she spoke with such a strong and firm voice. "I need to tell you *the story*."

I found myself sitting in silence as Granny began telling *the story*. "The true story," Granny began as she looked out somewhere. I followed her gaze. "My life was just like my mother and her mother before her. Before leaving Skeldon, Guyana, I was able to sit and talk with my grandmother's suitor's son, Bryan, who I had befriended. He would have been your great-great-grandmother Philomena's stepson.

He helped me put the missing pieces together of that tragic Christmas Day that claimed the life of my grandmother Philomena."

I just sat there, wondering what else could Granny Gracie unpeel from this story that I've heard time and time again.

As I looked at Granny lying in the bed, she began to look different to me. She looked old, and it finally clicked that my anchor, my rock, was going to die. This thought caught me off guard because I always thought Granny Gracie was going to live on forever.

"Madeline," Granny called as she noticed her precious grandbaby in her own thoughts, "your great-great-grandmother Philomena's untimely death was by the hand of Big Jack's wife. Madeline, Philomena, my grandmother was a legend with men, and shortly after she conceived, she moved to Georgetown, Guyana. She ended up living in Georgetown for a number of years to raise her one and only daughter, Sophia, your great-grandmother until she reached adolescent age. When Jack found out that Philomena was pregnant, he desperately wanted to be with her, so he searched all over Skeldon for my grandmother, but he never found her. His heart ached for her, even though he was married. His wife knew in her soul that there was another woman even though her husband tried to mask it. On one of his business trips to Georgetown many years later, he could not believe his eyes when he saw them, Philomena and this beautiful little girl standing next to her. When Philomena turned and saw Jack, her heart leaped, for she was so happy to see him. They reconnected. She confessed why she had left Skeldon and her desire to return to finish the project of the waterline. Over the next few years, Jack traveled to Georgetown every week 'on business,' just so he could spend every moment with my grandmother." Granny's focus from nowhere is now intently on me.

"Skeldon was a small and devout Christian community, an intimate environment with very few single people. Philomena wasn't exceptionally attractive, but had a kind heart and would often find herself in a position of providing succor to the men who would call on her, but Jack was the man she loved. Philomena was on her way back to Skeldon. Jack's wife had gone to the station with the intent of confronting her husband, but instead she saw Philomena with him and she walked up to them and shot my grandmother, Philomena, at point-blank range while they were standing on Platform B at the Linden train station. Philomena didn't succumb to her injuries immediately but was transported back to Skeldon where she later died."

Granny Gracie went on. "Sophia was there and witnessed the brutal shooting. She became paralyzed with fear, so much so that her memory of the shooting was obscured, distancing the reality of the tragedy while replacing it with contrived pictures of her truth. She was only 12 when it happened. Dr. Jon Smider, the local doctor of Skeldon, took care of Sophia until she was 18 and able to care for herself."

Granny was silent, dazed, and looking really exhausted. "Madeline, unfortunately, my mother Sophia lived a life no different

than her mother before her. My mother also lived a life of having many suitors all of whom were married. Madeline, my mother died a spinster with ten bastard children. The visible scars are embedded in my memory of the many men that would come to the house to call on her. Many of whose children were my friends. They went to school with me. As I matured, I too found myself in similar relationships, too many to remember."

Granny then drifted off to sleep, right in the

middle of the story. As I started to get up, I guess the movement caused her to wake up, and she continued.

"Madeline, do you remember the story of the mechanism that my granny Philomena was going to introduce to Skeldon?" Granny asked. "I'm trying to remember, Granny——the mechanism," I answered.

I was as clueless as Nicodemus trying to understand how to become a child again in order to enter into the kingdom of God.[3]

"Granny, please get some rest," I requested. My concern for Granny heightened. "Granny, I'm going to call for help. You need to go to the hospital!" I exclaimed.

Just as I was about to leave for help, Granny said, "No, I probably need just another cup of tea, and it can wait! Please get the Bible off the nightstand and turn it to the Gospel of John, the fourth chapter, and begin reading from verse seven."

I opened the Bible and began reading from verse seven:

> *When a Samaritan woman came to draw water, Jesus said to her, "Will you give me a drink?" (His disciples had gone into the town to buy food.) The Samaritan woman said to him, "You are a Jew, and I am a Samaritan woman. How can you ask me for a drink?" (For Jews do not associate with Samaritans.) Jesus*

---

[3] John 3:4, NIV

The Woman At The Well

answered her, "If you knew the gift of God and who it is that asks you for a drink, you would have asked him, and he would have given you living water." "Sir," the woman said, "you have nothing to draw with, and the well is deep. Where can you get this living water? Are you greater than our father Jacob, who gave us the well and drank from it himself, as did also his sons and his livestock?" Jesus answered, "Everyone who drinks this water will be thirsty again, but whoever drinks the water I give them will never thirst. Indeed, the water I give them will become in them a spring of water welling up to eternal life." The woman said to him, "Sir, give me this water so that I won't get thirsty and have to keep coming here to draw water." He told her, "Go, call your husband and come back." "I have no husband," she replied. Jesus said to her, "You are right when you say you have no husband. The fact is, you have had five husbands, and the man you now have is not your husband. What you have just said is quite true." "Sir," the woman said, "I can see that you are a prophet. Our ancestors worshiped on this mountain, but you Jews claim that the place where

> *we must worship is in Jerusalem." "Woman," Jesus replied, "believe me, a time is coming when you will worship the Father neither on this mountain nor in Jerusalem. You Samaritans worship what you do not know; we worship what we do know, for salvation is from the Jews. Yet a time is coming and has now come when the true worshipers will worship the Father in the Spirit and in truth, for they are the kind of worshipers the Father seeks. God is spirit, and his worshipers must worship in the Spirit and in truth." The woman said, "I know that Messiah" (called Christ) "is coming. When he comes, he will explain everything to us." Then Jesus declared, "I, the one speaking to you—I am he.[4]"*

I closed the Bible and looked at Granny as she continued with *the story*.

"Madeline, I was like the woman at the well. The woman at the well had many husbands, but Jesus pointed out to her that the one that she was with wasn't her husband either, they all belonged to other women. Because of her behavior, she would only come to the

---

[4] John 4:7–26

The Woman At The Well

well at the height of day to draw water. After all the other women had made the trip. Now she found herself in conversation with a Jewish man, no doubt probably saw him as a possible suitor."

"Granny Gracie!" I shouted.

Granny had that mischievous twinkle in her eyes. Granny continued. "He was a Jew and she was a Samaritan. A woman by her mere actions was excluded from her community. This Jewish man could tell her everything about the life she lived. He never condemned her, criticized her, or ostracized her. He offered the woman at the well hope, forgiveness and an invitation to drink from the well with a mechanism that would cause her to find the true gift of self-worth and self-forgiveness, to enable her to enjoy a life of eternal forgiveness for every sin she had ever committed. That mechanism, Madeline, is *grace*. Only one who is driven by divine passion can consider doing something for someone without expecting something in return.

"Madeline, listen to me. I found myself ostracized from my community. Just like the woman in the story you just read, I had many men who had their own wives, something that I am not proud of. The Inglee women have carried the curse of adultery since I can remember. When I had asked whether you remembered the mechanism, it was to be a symbol

> ***Lesson 10***
>
> *When we surrender our life to Him, we will eventually find forgiveness in our heart and peace within the soul.*

for the Inglee women to break the curse. Just like the woman at the well, Jesus was offering her grace or a platform of forgiveness. That is something that goes beyond the natural man's ability to accept or comprehend, and it is something only He can offer. Your great-great-grandmother Philomena wanted desperately to be accepted as part of the Skeldon community, but she never fitted in. She was originally from Suriname, an outsider to Skeldon. She was unmarried. In the community where she moved into, everyone was married. She had fallen in love with the beauty of Skeldon and the possibilities of a better life than what she remembered she had in Suriname. Shortsightedness should have aroused her intuition, a single woman in a land of married people, but it didn't, as opportunity was her main focus. It wasn't long before her desires dictated her actions. Philomena knew God, but she fell victim to lust with the only means of relief, as she was convinced, was with the married men of her community. Philomena assumed because she fell from God's grace she couldn't be restored back to Him. Her promiscuous living would then become the root that connected and determined the lives of her children and their children to come. Philomena wanted so badly to build the water infrastructure in Skeldon, that she couldn't see the symbolic message God was giving her with that vision. She went to Georgetown in search of the dipping apparatus, but God was offering it to her all along, Madeline, He was offering her grace! It was the only thing that could set us free from bondage and now, you have it. My mother, Sophia, built the

The Woman At The Well

infrastructure by birthing me and my nine siblings. My dear Caroline gave way to the dipping device that lies in you." You will break the curse on the Inglee women.

Before dozing off again, Granny whispered, "Madeline, you must realize that you are special."

For the past hour, Granny seemed to be falling in and out of sleep. Oddly strange, I thought. Perhaps it's due to her age. Maybe it was the trapped gas she was feeling.

As I looked out of the bedroom window, the sky had become pitch- black; there was not a star in the sky. I remembered Granny saying, *"Madeline, when the sky is dark and without stars, rain is in the air, plus the fact,"* she would say, *"my bunion on my left foot and the corn on my baby toe on my right foot is aching."* The thought made me chuckle as the rain was pattering on the window pane.

My life seemed to be full of rain as of late. The invisible force seemed more prevalent now than it did back in my dream. The dream, I hadn't thought about the dream in years.

"Why now?" I wondered.

Again, I looked at Granny Gracie, she really wasn't looking well.

Musalem was out in the dining room, and I asked him to please arrange to get Granny to the hospital. As we waited for the ambulance, I suddenly realized that Granny was the only person left in my life. My mother was dead and Granny was dying. As the rain pelted the windowpane, the same were the tears quietly pouring from my eyes.

I was so tired and so I curled up in the bed with

Granny. I found my-self in an unfamiliar place, speaking to the invisible force, asking it to please protect Granny. Granny awakened as she felt my body next to her.

"Madeline, please sit up, dear. I have to tell you the story," she whispered. "Do you remember the dream you had a few years ago?"

Granny asked.

I was so overwhelmed with pain just thinking about Granny dying, that I almost missed the question.

"Yes, Granny," I answered.

"Madeline, after you were born, I found myself at my lowest. Your mother was the result of one of my indiscretions. I raised her with a hope that she would live a life more meaningful than I ever had. Your mother showed great promise until that dreadful day, May 24. I had left your mother at home alone, something I still regret to this day." She took a deep breath.

"Your mother, Madeline, was raped by Nahshon."

There were still portions of Granny's life that she still would not bring herself to tell.

"Madeline, Musalem is your brother." "What are you saying, Granny?"

My heart began beating so hard against my chest. The room was spinning. I couldn't breathe. My breathing began to pulsate like I was having a heart attack. I grabbed my chest.

"Granny, I can't breathe!" I cried.

"Madeline, please listen to me, take some deep breaths, hold my hand," Granny said.

I collapsed in Granny's bed now crying uncontrollably. "Madeline, Madeline," Granny whispered, "I don't have much time."

I need you to know like the woman at the well. You have been extended an invitation to drink the water, salvation, with the *new mechanism* and that is grace, which is extended to those who desire to feel true agape love and forgiveness that only Jesus Christ can give. The Bible shows that it is a simple process. If you declare with your mouth *'Jesus is Lord,' and believe in your heart that God raised him from the dead, you will be saved. For it is with your heart that you believe and are justified, and it is with your mouth that you profess your faith and are saved.*[5]"

Granny Gracie found the strength to sit up in the bed and cupped both of my hands in hers as she asked, "Madeline, will you accept Jesus as your personal Savior today? Promise me that you will honor God with your life and your living. For when you do, agape love and forgiveness will fill your heart!"

I answered her between the sobs, "Yes, I will." I noticed Granny's breathing was a bit labored.

"Madeline, you are God's chosen vessel. Commit your ways to him and he will protect you from yourself. Let us pray. Father God, I submit to you my granddaughter, the last of the Inglee women. Please break the curse of adultery, in the name of Jesus I pray. Amen."

Granny took what seemed like the deepest breath

---

[5] Romans 10:9–10

ever. As Musalem entered the room with the ambulance attendant, he could hear Madeline crying hysterically, "Granny, Granny, please, God, do not take my granny too!"

Granny Gracie was buried at St. Joseph's Graveyard in St. George's.

My thoughts hadn't been clear since my grandmother's last words, *"Nahshon is your father."*

With mixed emotions of anger and hate, I decided, at 23 years of life, it would be best to leave the only home I knew. I would leave Bermuda and move back to where it all started for the Inglee family— Suriname.

> ***Lesson 11***
>
> *The precipice of truth enables fortitude. Do not allow mistruths to keep you in bondage.*

~

CHAPTER 8

It had been three weeks since Granny's death when I bumped into Musalem at the market. Uncertain if or how to approach me, Musalem pretended not to see me in the dry goods aisle. Musalem was well aware that I was his sister, his father had revealed to him the whole story, rape and all. He realized that there was an incredible bond between him and I, only to his amazement. The bond was biological.

Musalem desperately desired our relationship to be as it was before Granny Gracie died.

> **Lesson 12**
>
> *Life in its purest sense is experienced when grace and mercy has been accepted.*

I looked at Musalem dead in the eye and gave a

brief, but abrupt, greeting while pushing my grocery cart past him as quickly as I could. I couldn't stand to look at him or maybe I angry with his father. I never confessed Nahshon as my father. My emotions where running wild.

"Why me?" I whispered to myself. Now, I had no one.

As I approached the cashier, Musalem was already checking out. He so missed his friend and wanted to somehow rekindle their friendship. "Lin, how are you, really?" he asked.

"I'm doing as well as expected," I replied. "Can we talk?" he asked.

I quickly started to reminisce about all of the talks and secrets we shared. Musalem was approximately two years younger than me and for the first time, I noticed that we shared the same dark brown eyes with midnight black hair. Our skin tone was the color of golden brown wheat bread. Madeline began to see Musalem as a brother and a friend.

"Musalem, I would be happy to get together. We can meet at Granny's house. How about later today?"

"That would be fine with me," replied Musalem.

I had already started the process of packing up Granny's house for my intended relocation to Suriname. I hadn't confirmed the date, but was sure that it was pointless to remain in the house. My plan to sell the house would provide the money needed to begin a new life.

There was a knock at the door. It was Musalem, waiting to be invited into the house. Typically, when Granny was alive, Musalem would knock and enter.

The Woman At The Well

Things were so different since Granny died.

Granny's house was of modest décor, and when you entered the house, you walked into the grand sunroom with its noticeably large bay windows that allowed for natural light to accentuate the greenery Granny had throughout the house. I had inherited Granny's green thumb. Every plant was lush, green, and in bloom. I had modestly set the side hutch with Granny's porcelain china, variety of teas, crumpets, and pastries, which I had prepared only the day before. I invited Musalem to join me in the parlor. He was amazed at how much I was like Granny, so much so that he anticipated Granny to walk out into the parlor and join us at any moment.

"Are these all Granny's things that are in the boxes?" Musalem asked.

"No, not all," I replied.

"Not all?" Musalem asked in a puzzled tone. "No, some are mine," I replied.

"You are leaving?" he asked.

I poured him a cup of tea and sat back while contemplating my response. "Musalem, a lot has happened. Granny's story . . ." My gaze began to drift. "It's too much for me to comprehend. How do you accept such betrayal? How do you forgive someone of such a horrendous act? Your father raped my mother! And she had the nerve to want me to acknowledge him as uncle!"

Musalem responded, "But he's your father too!"

"Listen, Musalem, you have always been kind and generous to me. Wow! For God's sake, you are my brother! I wish Granny had kept that story and took it with her to her grave!" I began crying and shouting at the top of my lungs.

Musalem calmly placed his teacup on the saucer. He reached for my hand. "Lin, I am so sorry for how you are feeling. I also felt angry and happy at the same time."

I gave him the Inglee look. "What are you saying, Musalem?" I asked.

"Lin, deep down in my heart, I always wished that if I had a sister she would be just like you. You are so special. You have the kindest heart I've ever known anyone to have. You know what to say at the right time. You remember the time I had my first, let's say, indiscretion, I came to you and you not only helped me through it, but you also prayed for me. Do you remember that?"

I began to reflect. "Yes, I do remember," I said.

"I went to Granny Gracie to ask her why you seem to have God's anointing over your life as my life felt like a living hell!" Musalem declared. "I cried and asked Granny if I was being punished for my father's actions. Lin, I told Granny that I hated my father, especially for what he did to your mother. Granny sat me down and had me read from her Bible, John 4:7–26."

Musalem could hardly finish his sentence when I chimed in. "That's the same scripture I read for her just before she died!" I exclaimed. "She told me that the scripture was designed to break the Inglee curse of adultery and it would free me from judging people, but to love and forgive them as Christ forgave the woman at the well."

The Woman At The Well

"Musalem, what is happening?" I asked as I slumped into the wingback chair.

"Lin, all I can say is that the hand of God has been on you since I can remember. You have been called for a purpose. I don't know what it is, but you are definitely special," he explained. "Listen, I don't know why you are running away. Your place is here, in this community. There is plenty of work to be done by you and me for God's Kingdom. Why and what are you running from? I have known you all of your life. The story that Granny shared with you, although upsetting . . ., but I know you, you are a person to rise above anything and everything that is thrown at you. Lin, why do you feel you have to leave?" he asked.

I listened to Musalem, but my spirit took me back to that weird dream I had as a young girl.

"Musalem, I have to share some-thing with you. I never quite understood what it meant. It's about a dream I had many years ago.

> **Lesson 13**
>
> *Own your history, stop running from it, and learn from it.*

"It was dusk. The area was unfamiliar to me, people were running everywhere. I began to run 'cause everyone else was running. There was something in the distance. I couldn't readily make it out. Then as it got closer. It had a sunset-colored glow and it looked like a huge tumbleweed on fire. It consumed everything in its way and then it was on me. It was hot, but it didn't burn me. It had a firm grip, but it didn't hurt me. I was on fire, but nothing on me burned, nor did I smell like smoke. Then I heard a voice. I'll never forget the sound. It said, *'I am that I am. Madeline, I have called you to be an agent for me. I am the Alpha and the Omega, the beginning and the end.'"* I stopped speaking. There was a deathly silence in the room.

Musalem immediately had an interpretation of the dream. "Lin," he said so quietly that I could barely hear him, "as believers of Christ, we can spend years following the commands of the Bible and not receive a revelatory word or even a visit from the Holy Spirit. You had an encounter with the Holy Spirit. Such an encounter only comes when one has found favor in the sight of God. God looks at the heart of man, not for the good works that he does, but because they have a desire to serve him."

I looked at Musalem as if he had just lost his mind. "Musalem, I don't even go to church!" I chuckled.

"Lin, the manifestation of the Holy Spirit in one's life has little to do with if you attend church. Turn with me to 1 Samuel 3:1–10. Read with me," Musalem suggested.

> *The boy Samuel ministered before the Lord under Eli. In those days, the word of the Lord was rare; there were not many visions. One night Eli, whose eyes were becoming so weak that he could barely see, was lying down in his usual place. The lamp of God had not yet gone out, and Samuel was lying down in*

The Woman At The Well

the house of the Lord, where the ark of God was. Then the Lord called Samuel. Samuel answered, "Here I am." And he ran to Eli and said, "Here I am you called me." But Eli said, "I did not call go back and lie down." So he went and lay down. Again, the Lord called, "Samuel!" And Samuel got up and went to Eli and said, "Here I am you called me." "My son," Eli said, "I did not call go back and lie down." Now Samuel did not yet know the Lord. The word of the Lord had not yet been revealed to him. A third time the Lord called, "Samuel!" And Samuel got up and went to Eli and said, "Here I am you called me." Then Eli realized that the Lord was calling the boy. So, Eli told Samuel, "Go and lie down, and if he calls you, say, 'Speak, Lord, for your servant is listening.'" So Samuel went and lay down in his place. The Lord came and stood there, calling as at the other times, "Samuel! Samuel!" Then Samuel said, "Speak, for your servant is listening."[6]

We both closed the Bible simultaneously. Musalem began the conversation. "Lin, Samuel

---

[6] 1 Samuel 3:1–10

received a call from God at a time when a prophetic word or vision from the Lord was rare and, also, before he even knew or understood the voice of the Lord. By Eli's time, no prophets were speaking God's messages to Israel. Why? Due to the boastful attitude of Eli's sons. When persons made offerings in order that their sins might be forgiven, Eli's sons would steal the offering and then make a mockery of the people's repentance. They even took the ark into battle thinking it would protect them, however God withdrew his protection. In other words, Lin, Eli's sons did some dumb stuff. Here's the catch — Eli was aware. Eli was the high priest ignoring the sins of the priests (his sons) under his jurisdiction. Because his sons refused to listen to God and allowed greed to get in the way of any communication coupled with Eli's disregarding their behavior, helped to facilitate a prophetic hush throughout the land. In other words, Lin, they knew right from wrong, but blatantly ignored their teachings. So, in the silence when Samuel kept coming to Eli, Eli had become unfamiliar with the voice of God, hence his delayed instruction to Samuel."[7]

I began to reflect on granny's story. *"The Inglee women were all raised in the Christian faith, but allowed adultery to get in the way of any communication with God. This is starting to make sense,"* I thought.

---

[7] New International Version Life Application Interpretation—1 Samuel 3:1-5

Musalem cleared his throat to recapture my attention. "Lin, listening, responding and remaining humble is vital in a

> **Lesson 14**
>
> *Accept the saving knowledge of Jesus Christ and move freely in your predestined purpose.*

relationship with God. He spoke and anointed you for his service. God called you, he spoke to you. '*I am that I am.*

Madeline, I have called you to be an agent for me. I am the Alpha and the Omega, the beginning and the end.' He called you to action, Madeline, to engage in being a beacon of light for Him, by spreading the gospel of Jesus Christ to everyone you come into contact. Have you heard his voice, lately?" Musalem asked.

I replied, "No, I don't think so."

"Next time that he calls you— and, Lin, he will— answer him like Samuel did, *'Speak Lord for your servant is listening,'*" Musalem suggested.

At that point, I-began to feel the presence of the invisible force. There was a warmth that engulfed me. Strangely, I wasn't afraid and had no desire to run. Musalem noticed a shift in my demeanor.

"Lin, want to share?" he asked.

I looked at him with a bewildered look, "I think it is speaking right now," I whispered.

"You know what to do," replied Musalem.

At that moment, I made up my mind that I would surrender. I opened my mouth and, with tears running down my cheeks, said,

"Dear Father, I am so sorry for being angry and not wanting to forgive you for taking Granny and then angry because of the Inglee history. I do believe that I am created in your image and that your Son Jesus died for my sins. I no longer have to feel like the victim. I accept you as Lord over my life. I love you, Lord Jesus. So here I am with all my faults, I surrender me to you."

And that I did. I believed in my heart that I was called for a purpose and spoke to the invisible force, just as Samuel did. "Speak, Lord, for your servant is listening."

~

CHAPTER 9

Several months had passed since my renewal experience. I still followed my decision to visit both places of my heritage, Suriname and Skeldon. I stayed in Suriname for a short while as I inquired about the Inglee family name. To travel the original path of my great-great-grandmother's legacy was a tremendous eye-opener. Through the records office in Paramaribo, I discovered my great-great-great grandparents, Iglesias Martinez Inglee and Cassandra Marandez Lopiez Abraham, had two descendants; Philomena Cassandra Marandez and Phillipe Martinez who originated from the village of Apetina located near the jungle. It was not conducive for me to travel to Apetina due to the unfinished roads that led to the area. I decided to continue my search in Skeldon, Guyana.

When I arrived in Skeldon, it seemed uncannily familiar. I quickly concluded it must have been due to the stories Granny Gracie had shared with me. Skeldon had become a very progressive city, with running water flowing throughout the city and to think that it was her grandmother's tenacity that brought it into fruition.

Some things in Skeldon hadn't changed in years. One was when a new face came into town it was quickly noticed and would cause a buzz of inquisitiveness in the community. When I walked into the motel and announced my name, Rosa, the front-desk personnel, quickly recognized the significance of the Inglee name.

"Good afternoon, Ms. Inglee, and welcome to the Skeldon Motel.

My name is Rosa. Allow me to show you to your room," said Rosa.

Rosa was the niece of Grace Philomena Inglee. Her mother Liza had often shared with her daughter the possibilities of reaching higher heights like her sister Gracie had. The story was told how Gracie set sail on the *Bermuda Veselle*, opting for a better life than Skeldon. Liza was the youngest and the only living sibling of Gracie. Liza had done well in the community. The Skeldon Motel was her business and had provided a comfortable livelihood for her and Rosa.

As an astute businesswoman, Liza realized that she had made no provision for a recipient of her legacy. She was 38 years old and motherless. Her work ethic left no space for meaningful relationships until she met Henry Mitchel Smider. When Liza was in her prime, she would turn the head of every person she

The Woman At The Well

would pass by. She was very poised, well-dressed, and an extremely attractive woman. Henry was recommended by her executive assistant as a person she should consider putting on the development board for her motel. Henry brought a wealth of experience to the development of having facilitated numerous building projects in the neighboring country of Trinidad and Tobago.

It did not take long before Henry and Liza had kindled a private relationship. Liza was adamant that she remained focused on bringing the dream of opening the motel on schedule. She had been in several one-night relationships, but Henry seemed to understand her. He respected her as a strong woman and, most important, he was able to fulfill her desires. Their relationship had bloomed into something truly special until the New Year's open gala. They were to meet at the gala and she would tell him that she was carrying their child. When Liza arrived at the gala, she radiated the room. Her long, dark brown hair flowed in the recess of her bosom. Everything about Liza was perfect and gorgeous. Her figure was perfect and the rose-colored, soft, silk dress clung to her like the skin of a banana. The hump in her belly was not that noticeable. Every head turned as she walked on to the ballroom floor. It was then that she saw him talking with a group of people unfamiliar to her. She noticed a woman that seemed to be standing very close to Henry. As she began to approach the group, Henry turned toward her. His eyes spoke volumes.

He said without speaking, "Stay where you are."

Liza looked every bit confused as he walked across the dance floor. He gently grasped her elbow as he walked her toward the exit.

"Liza, I'm sorry. There is something I should have told you," he whispered. As he began to speak, Liza closed her eyes ever so tightly. "I am married," he said.

And with all her strength and dignity she replied, "And I am carrying your child." She turned and left the gala.

Liza understood the struggle of her mother Sophia and vowed to never be caught in a similar situation — husbandless with several children. But here she was, husbandless and at least with one child on the way.

Although Liza was viewed within her community as an astute businesswoman, she had a very soft side to her personality and that is why she loved Henry because he complemented her. Unfortunately, he exploited that sensitivity. She was determined to raise her child without Henry and to redirect all her energy back into the building project.

When Rosa was born, Liza did all she could to protect her from falling in the trappings of dishonest relationships. Rosa was special. She had a countenance that radiated love, a love different from the Inglee traditions. She had a free spirit, but was very attuned to any spirit that did not represent honor, wholeness, or goodness. Rosa loved life, loved her mother and family.

Over the years, Liza had often told Rosa that God will send an Inglee back to Skeldon to help break the curse of adultery and lustful pleasures. Rosa could not

The Woman At The Well

wait to go and tell her mother that a Madeline Inglee had just checked into the motel.

After I was checked in and settled, I decided to go and see if I could find any connection to my family. I ventured out on Skandon Street where I found a large department store and I entered to browse around. Near the housewares department were very old pictures of two stately looking women. They looked oddly familiar, and then the sales lady interrupted my thoughts. "Hello, may I help you with anything?"

I responded, "No, thanks. I'm just looking."

My accent gave me away as the sales lady probed, "Are you visiting, Skeldon?"

"Yes, I am," I replied. Somehow, I didn't feel comfortable completely sharing my purpose with her.

"Hi, my name is Liz, short for Elizabeth. And your name is?" she said all in one breath.

"My name is Madeline."

"I noticed that you were staring at the photos on the wall. She was the owner and founder of this store. She was my great-great-grandma, Philomena Inglee, and the other lady was her daughter, Sophia Inglee, my great-grandma," Liz categorically stated. "Well, Madeline, I would like to be the first to extend an invitation to come to Sensuality," Liz said.

"Sensuality! What is Sensuality?" I asked.

"Oh, the name can be deceiving. It's the night club here in town." "Thank you for the invitation, but I will have to respectfully decline,"

I responded as I decided that it was time to leave the store. As I headed toward the motel, I refocused on Liz's statement. *"She was my great-great-grandma, Philomena, and my great-grandma, Sophia ... Had I just met a cousin?"* I thought.

At first chance, Rosa raced home to tell her mother about the new guest that had just checked into the motel. "Mom, a Madeline Inglee just checked into the motel!" she exclaimed. Liza turned and looked at her daughter and asked her to repeat what she had just said.

> **Lesson 15**
>
> *Exercised faith can make the impossible possible.*

"A Madeline Inglee just checked into the motel," she repeated. "We must go to the motel," declared Liza.

They left immediately.

When Liza and Rosa arrived at the motel, I was just returning from my walk-about. Although Liza hadn't seen her sister Gracie in years, you would have thought that she had just walked through the motel doors. Liza was stunned. Madeline not only looked like Gracie, but her very countenance was also like Gracie.

I felt a bit uncomfortable as I realized the lady behind the counter next to Rosa was staring at me very intently. Rosa broke the tension by introducing me to her mom. "Madeline, please meet Liza . . . Liza Inglee!" said Rosa.

I couldn't believe her ears. "You said Liza Inglee," I all but whispered.

"Yes, I am Liza Inglee, daughter of the late Sophia Cassandra Inglee," replied Liza.

"Aunt Liza!" I could hardly contain myself as I went behind the counter to embrace them. What would be the odds of meeting my relatives right in the motel where I was staying?

We talked and shared to the early hours of the next day. When I retreated to my room, I thought, this was a great start, as I drifted off to sleep.

~

CHAPTER 10

As Liza opened her eyes as the mark of a new day, she dropped on her knees and gave thanks to God for answering her prayer. "*The work can now begin,*" she concluded in her thoughts.

When Gracie left Skeldon over 70 years ago, Liza just knew in her heart that God would send an Inglee back to help the family. Liza, although the last child of Sophia, had experienced a great deal, and by the time Liza was in her early teens, Sophia took exceptional notice of her daughter. She was different from her other children. Liza had a beautiful spirit. She would always look out for the well-being of her mother, where her other siblings grew and grew out of the family home and never looked back. The birth of Liza seemed to be the healing that Sophia so longed for after her mother's death. It all came together;

The Woman At The Well

Sophia was a broken woman. Her very spirit was broken from a young age. She was motherless and had latched on to everyone else's husband to fill the void in her life, and then came Gracie. Sophia truly loved Gracie, as she was her firstborn. However, Sophia's life still remained empty. Gracie was beautiful, but she couldn't complete the brokenness that Sophia experienced.

By the time Liza was born, Sophia began to find peace. It was one Sunday after Liza had been to church that she invited her mother to read with her John 4:7-26,

> *When a Samaritan woman came to draw water, Jesus said to her, "Will you give me a drink?" (His disciples had gone into the town to buy food.) The Samaritan woman said to him, "You are a Jew and I am a Samaritan woman. How can you ask me for a drink?" (For Jews do not associate with Samaritans.) Jesus answered her, "If you knew the gift of God and who it is that asks you for a drink, you would have asked him and he would have given you living water." "Sir," the woman said, "you have nothing to draw with, and the well is deep. Where can you get this living water? Are you greater than our father Jacob, who gave us the well and drank from it himself, as did also his sons and his livestock?" Jesus answered,*

"Everyone who drinks this water will be thirsty again, but whoever drinks the water I give them will never thirst. Indeed, the water I give them will become in them a spring of water welling up to eternal life." The woman said to him, "Sir, give me this water so that I won't get thirsty and have to keep coming here to draw water." He told her, "Go, call your husband and come back." "I have no husband," she replied. Jesus said to her, "You are right when you say you have no husband. The fact is you have had five husbands, and the man you now have is not your husband. What you have just said is quite true." "Sir," the woman said, "I can see that you are a prophet. Our ancestors worshiped on this mountain, but you Jews claim that the place where we must worship is in Jerusalem." "Woman," Jesus replied, "believe me, a time is coming when you will worship the Father neither on this mountain nor in Jerusalem. You Samaritans worship what you do not know. We worship what we do know, for salvation is from the Jews. Yet a time is coming and has now come when the true worshipers will worship the Father in the Spirit and in truth, for they are the kind of worshipers the Father seeks. God is

spirit, and his worshipers must worship in the Spirit and in truth." The woman said, "I know that Messiah" (called Christ) "is coming. When he comes, he will explain everything to us." Then Jesus declared, "I, the one speaking to you—I am he."[8]

Liza immediately noticed a shift in her mother's countenance. "Mommy," Liza said, "why not accept the grace that can only be offered at the well? You have often told me the stories of the gadget your mom sought to get in Georgetown, but I believe that Grandma Philomena was doing a natural task with a hope of bringing spiritual healing to herself, but more importantly, Mommy, I believe that she was looking out for you. She knew you had the ability to make the difference in your home and community. Mommy, accept Jesus today and allow his grace to heal all your hurts and fulfill your needs."

Sophia accepted. Life changed for her and her relationship with Liza only blossomed. When Liza gave birth to Rosa, Sophia knew that the goodness that was in her daughter Liza was in her beautiful granddaughter Rosa. She truly loved her granddaughter. Sophia would hope that what Liza and Rosa experienced, her other children and grandchildren would find that same inner peace.

---

[8] John 4:7–26

When Sophia passed, her children and their children showed up to the family homestead. Although Liza loved her family, she couldn't stand their waywardness, self-centeredness, and the corrupt way in which they lived. Liza found herself praying often for her family, that by the grace of God, they too would find that there was another way to live.

Rosa had already left for the motel, as she was just as excited to have met her cousin Madeline. She wanted to know about her home, Bermuda, and if it was as beautiful as the magazines described it.

When Rosa arrived, Madeline was sitting in the sunroom where she was having breakfast.

"Good morning, Madeline," said Rosa.

"And a good morning to you," I replied.

As they had engaged in small pleasantries, Liza arrived. "Good morning, dear. It is a wonderful morning to give thanks," she beckoned to both me and Rosa.

After sitting, Liza looked to the heavens as if she was acknowledging a special presence. "Madeline, I, or we, have been praying for this moment for a long while, that God will send an Inglee back to Skeldon to break the generational curse of this family. We have lived a life contrary to what Grandma Philomena would have wanted, but we know and believe that the rest of our family can receive the grace that has been extended to us by way of salvation. Despite the wrongs we have done in thought, word, or deed, when you declare with your mouth *Jesus is Lord and believe in your heart that God raised him from the dead, you will be saved. For it is with your heart that you believe and*

The Woman At The Well

are justified, and it is with your mouth that you profess your faith and are saved."[9]

Let us therefore, pray and believe that Jesus Christ will break the generational curse for our family and all families and that He will also forgive us all and restore our families back to Him, Amen."

When they prayed, Elizabeth, the sales lady from the department store, walked into the sunroom, looking for Aunt Liza, with tears rolling down her cheeks.

"Aunt Liza, please help me?" Elizabeth asked as the tears billowed from her eyes.

"Today, when I woke up I realized that I have to do something different. I'm tired of the drinking, the bad abusive relationships I continually get involved with. Aunt Liza, help me, please?" Elizabeth pleaded. She then caught glimpse of the lady from the store. "It's you, you're Madeline, how do you know my Aunt Liza?" she said all in one breath.

Aunt Liza said, "Let's pray."

I and Rosa glanced at each other while Aunt Liza began to pray.

> **Lesson 16**
>
> *Fervent prayer delivers, heals, and restores the soul.*

The healing process had begun. To God be the glory!

~

---

[9] Romans 10:9–10

Epilogue

Forgiveness still remains the catalyst for healing. It is a self-imposed process. To forgive oneself of inflicted travesty, emotional betrayal, and compromised self-worth will ultimately allow the soul to be restored to the acclaimed and predestined place God originally intended, as we are created in his image.

However, we are so accustomed to suppressing past hurts and deliberate violation of self-worth because we must appear to live a life reflective of wholesome living. How then does the healing begin? Life says swallow it and live with it when the soul cries for help and, most times, relief.

This allegory of the woman at the well perpetrates the story of all who live their life's lie as truth. The story depicts generational curses, such as adultery, promiscuity, and deceit. However, there are many other contributors to the actions we engage that denounce the glory of God, to which we are all called to exemplify.

Therefore, seek forgiveness so that your healing can begin, then the restoration process of entering into the well, which is grace; the designed space of refuge that is God's mercy can be gained. The opportunity to experience God's agape love and salvation is freely offered when you truly seek after it.

And Jesus answered, "But whoever drinks the water I give them will never thirst. Indeed, the water I give them will become in them a spring of water welling up to eternal life." The woman said to him, "Sir, give me this water . . ."

THE END

INDEX

A

Abraham, Cassandra Lopiez, 61 activity, 26, 33, 35
agent, 45, 57, 59
Albert (governor's aide), 27–28, 30–31, 34
Alpha and Omega, 45, 57, 59
Apetina (village), 61

B

basement, 41
beach, 43–44
Bermuda, 25–26, 28, 30–33, 37, 43, 53, 68
Bermuda Islands, 19, 25
Bible, 9, 34, 48–49, 52, 56–58
blood, 31
Briden (Christian lady), 40–41 Bultner, Absalom, 33–35
business, 20, 24, 33, 62

C

child, 22, 24, 41, 47–48, 62–63, 66
children, 17, 24, 48, 51, 63, 66, 68
community, 20–21, 24, 26, 33, 40, 50–51, 56, 61–63, 68
countenance, 63–64

D

dance, 27, 29
Deacon Brown, 40–42
Deacon Mitchel, 41–42
development, 20, 62
distance, 21, 23, 28, 38, 45, 57
dream, 20, 25, 44–45, 51, 57, 62
drinks, 29, 48–50, 52, 66

E

ears, 28, 30, 64
Eli, 57–58
Elizabeth (saleslady), 63, 69

F

faith, 37–38, 52, 68
family, 17, 20–21, 41, 63, 66, 68–69
First Bank of Skeldon, 20 foot, 45
forgiveness, 9, 18, 35, 50, 52, 71

G

genocide, 20
Georgetown (Guyana), 19–20, 22, 47, 67
governor's ball, 27
grace, 50–52, 54, 67–68, 71
graduation, 37
granny. *See* Inglee, Gracie Philomena
Guyana, 19–20, 25, 28, 46–47, 61

H

heart attack, 37, 52
heaven, 19, 25, 68
hell, 41, 44
Henry, 62–63
Holy Spirit, 5, 45, 57
home, 21, 23, 26, 29–30, 33, 36–38, 41, 52–53, 68
honor, 11, 23, 63
hospital, 32, 35, 48, 51

I

Inglee, Caroline Sophia, 34–40 Inglee, Gracie Philomena, 17, 25–40, 44–46, 48, 50–51, 53, 55–56, 59, 61–62, 64, 66
Inglee, Iglesias Martinez, 61 Inglee, Liza, 62–64, 66–68
Inglee, Madeline Caroline, 18, 34,

40, 44–48, 50–57, 59, 61,
63–65, 68–69
Inglee, Philomena Cassandra, 17, 19–23, 34, 47–48, 51, 61
Inglee, Rosa, 61–64, 68
Inglee, Sophia Cassandra, 17, 19,

J

Jerusalem, 49, 67
23–24, 34, 47, 66, 68
invitation, 50, 52, 64
Jesus Christ, 48–50, 52, 59, 66–69
Jews, 49–50, 66–67
Jones, Claudia, 35–36
Jones, Musalem Bultner, 42, 44–46,
51–55, 57, 59
Jones, Nahshon Bultner, 35–36, 38–42, 44, 52

L

Lightning Tabernacle Church, 33–35, 37–38, 41, 46
Lin, 18, 36–38, 40, 45, 54, 56–59.
See also Inglee, Caroline Sophia
Lord, 5, 44, 57–60
Lucille (wealthy individual), 24

M

market, 26, 54
marriage, 36, 41
mechanism, 48, 50
memory, 46, 48
merchants, 21
mind, 39, 43–45, 57, 59
ministry, 33–36, 38–39
money, 20, 55
moon, 25
morning, 68
motel, 61–65, 68
murder, 30

N

Natalie (Lightning Tabernacle member), 34

P

Parlor, 55
partnership, 36
Pastor Absalom, 36, 39
Pastor Bultner, 35–38
pleasantries, 36, 38, 68
police, 31–32
pregnancy, 40–41
psychopathy, 30

R

rain, 51
Reverend Nahshon. *See* Jones, Nahshon Bultner river, 45

S

salvation, 49, 52, 67–68, 71
sanctuary, 34, 38–39, 41
Sandyman, Jeffrey, 27–31, 34
sensuality, 33, 64
servant, 58–60
Skeldon (town), 19–21, 24–26, 28, 47–48, 61–63, 68
Skeldon Motel, 61–62
Smider, Phillip "Big Jack," 21–22, 47
Spirit and Faith Church Incorporated, 36–37
stars, 51
storm, 31
Straetor, William, 23–24 Straetor, William Scanlon Sr., 24 suitors, 23, 48, 50
sun, 25
sunroom, 68–69
Suriname, 20, 50, 53, 55, 61

T

Television, 43
Trinidad and Tobago (country), 62 truth, 18, 43, 48–49, 53, 67, 71

W

water, 48–50, 52, 66–67
wife, 18, 28, 40–41, 47

Connect with
DR. GEORGETTE V. PRIME-GODWIN

Follow Me

f @gpgimpact   📷 @gpgimpact

🐦 @gpgimpact   in @gpgimpact

For more info, visit
www.godwininternational.org

Also Available From
DR. GEORGETTE V. PRIME-GODWIN

ISBN: Softcover 978-1-942871-35-4

eBook 978-1-942871-41-5

War Baby is a fictional tale that rings with biblical truth. The characters depicted within the story are completely fictitious and illustrates the indigenous and inherent aptitude of mankind who has become inept at hearing truth; and when probability rings, find themselves living a mediocre and darkened life.

Available at
amazon.com

Also Available From
DR. GEORGETTE V. PRIME-GODWIN

ISBN: Softcover 978-1-942871-38-5

eBook 978-1-942871-40-8

This book embraces the Nehemiah strategy used to rebuild the walls and reform the people in 52 days. The journey for the participant will go beyond the 52 days, encouraging a renewed focus and relationship that demonstrates an outward manifestation of the glory of God.

It is a plenipotentiary feat to preside over the work of the wall! But we know, we can do all things through Christ that strengthens us.

Enjoy the journey!

Available at
amazon.com

www.ingramcontent.com/pod-product-compliance
Lightning Source LLC
Chambersburg PA
CBHW071528080526
44588CB00011B/1598